Say Goodnight, Grace Notes:
New and Corrected Poems

by
Jack McCarthy

**EM Press**

EM Press
709 Marion Street
Joliet, Illinois   60436
www.em-press.com

SAY GOODNIGHT, GRACENOTES:  NEW AND CORRECTED POEMS
Copyright © 2003 by Jack McCarthy.  All rights reserved.

See Page iii for special individual acknowledgments

Cover design by Gregory Harms
Photography by Heather Lose

Body text typeset by Michael Kadela in Garamond

**ISBN: 0-9708012-3-8**

Printed in The United States of America by Knowles Printing for EM Press, LLC.

FIRST PRINTING,  APRIL 2003

# DEDICATION

This book is dedicated to the women in my life: Megan, Kathleen, and Annie, who have asked for so little from me. To my wife Carol, who demanded poetry and has inspired so much of it. To my sisters, Judy and Hannah, who saw me at my worst and never gave up on me.

And to the audience at the Cantab Lounge, Central Square, Cambridge, and all the audiences who have been kind to me; to everyone who has ever said, "I *love* Jack McCarthy." You know who you are.

Jack McCarthy is one of the wonders of contemporary poetry. He writes--
and often performs--dazzling narratives full of wit and humor, sadness and
hard thinking. He should be cloned. —Stephen Dobyns


American Library Association BOOKLIST review, 4-1-03:

McCarthy has been writing poetry for decades, but not much came of it
until 10 years ago when he turned 50, married his second wife, and decided
to read his work at a Boston-area open-mike poetry night. McCarthy is now
not only a much-loved star in the performance poetry world, he's also a
vibrant and inspiriting poet on the page. A self-described working guy who
has battled a number of unhealthy addictions, McCarthy brings his
compelling experiences to his poetry with nimble humor, hard-won
wisdom, and a raconteur's knack for telling diabolically barbed stories. In
his admiring introduction, poet Thomas Lux praises McCarthy for his
"natural, unforced," voice, and for his unfailing lucidity, and indeed,
McCarthy is concrete, candid, personal, and utterly captivating. He's also
caustic, sexy, and smart. As he writes with wry insight about his boyhood,
Catholicism, the Red Sox, asteroids, his daughters, old cars, advertising, our
time as the "Golden Age of the Opinion," and his love for his wife, he
casually but resoundingly extrapolates invaluable lessons in living from each
memory, episode, observation, and meditation.—Donna Seaman

# INTRODUCTION

Jack McCarthy is a vital part of a very large, needed, and necessary community of writers and poets in America who have no affiliation with colleges and universities. McCarthy has served his art form. The only ambition he seems to have is to tell the truth as best he can in poems. His work is direct, plainspoken, colloquial, authentic, lucid. Lucid, lucid again. Meaning: accessible (although I like Billy Collins' term for this kind of poetry – "hospitable" – just as much) enough, meaning: complexity, textures, richness, reverberations, etc. Not meaning: too obvious, clichéd, easily paraphrased. Meaning: not being more afraid of being understood than afraid of being misunderstood. That kind of lucidity takes some guts. Have you ever considered how easy it is to be obscure? Have you ever wondered if obscurity is really often a cover up for arbitrariness? You won't have this problem with McCarthy's work. You'll hear a natural, unforced voice in his poems, like listening to your best friend talk to you – urgently, calmly – while looking you straight in the eye. Of course, the poem will be much more articulate and rhythmical and less redundant than your best friend. That's what good writing does: it creates a kind of illusion. If you are watching a play, for example, and you are conscious every minute that you are watching someone act and that you are watching a play, then most likely the actor is doing a poor job and most likely the writer too. You get lost in reading or listening to Jack McCarthy's poems. Lost in characters, the story, the voice – so human, so alive. His poems are hard not to read. Only a real poet has as much forgiveness, as much generosity, as much crankiness as McCarthy. Read this poet, now.

– Thomas Lux

Ring the bells that still can ring.
Forget your perfect offering.
There's a crack, a crack in everything.
That's how the light gets in.
That's how the light gets in.

Leonard Cohen

# Contents

# SUBSTANCES

Sometimes when it's my turn I say,
My name is Jack, and I'm
constitutionally a stranger
to moderation in any of its forms.
That scene in Aliens

when the little squidlike thing
flies across the room
and fastens on someone's mouth
and it'll never come off
without killing the person—

we're like that, except with us
the squid didn't really fly
across the room, we **sucked** it.
That's how it was with alcohol,
and when I started drinking

I started sucking
cigarettes, and from the bottom
of my heart loved every drag that
ever scummed the cilia of my lungs
with the resin of its residue.

The only way I could stop drinking
was to hook myself on meetings,
they gave shape to the day,
and it was at those meetings
I got onto coffee

and by the way, when the last smokers
in the USA are bounty-hunted down,
they'll find them at AA meetings.
Sometimes watching reruns of Cheers
I wonder how Sam Malone stays sober,

1

you never see *him* going to meetings;
but then it's obvious,
he's upgraded his addiction onto women.
Well a little shape to the day
never hurt anybody. You go Sam.

When I encountered coldness in
my first marriage I took up jogging,
like entering endorphin maintenance
to stave off heroine withdrawal; like
Mithridates, taking controlled doses of

known poisons; like lockjaw vaccination.
We are like birds, that in the winter
of pain migrate to Guatemala on the
wings of our substances; we are
incapable of residence, our essence

*is* long-distance flight, we dare
not risk the pain of owning anything;
even the paths of our migrations
are seasonal—and winter's never
more than nine months away.

I stopped drinking only when it
hurt too much to drink. I stopped
smoking when it interfered with
jogging. I stopped jogging
when the pain in my hips started

waking me up at night, for ice cream—
which had to go when my cholesterol
reached escape velocity. (I haven't
had my cholesterol tested since,
but it's been fine.)

Coffee and Canada Mints and the aspirin
I take for my hips are eating at
the lining of my stomach as I speak.
All my life I've borrowed from Peter
against my body to pay Paul

for my emotions and now Peter's
tracked me down and nailed
foreclosure to my door for
the fourteenth and final
mortgage on my organs

and all I can say is, *I gave*
*him a good run for his money.*
Soon the only thing left will be...
poetry. And maybe that's how it
was supposed to be, arcade of

substances that seem to ease
the pain; but all you're playing
is Whack-a-Mole, you bash it
here, it pops up there—
till suddenly you stumble on

the substance of your destiny
and understand at last
that all the pain
you ever gave the slip
was pain of **not *doing this***.

# TOUCH PASSES

*for my father*

I remember his
long touch passes
in the back yard,
thrown underhand

those last few years because
his arm wouldn't come over the top any more.
I'd run a fly
and the ball would spiral

lazy and high
and I'd swear it was uncatchable.
But if I maintained my
absolute top speed, such as it was

for twenty more yards
that old black swollen leather ball
would hang up in the dusk just long enough
that I could get my fingertips to it

and I had learned from him
if you could reach it you should catch it,
and though my lungs were fire,
my hands were glue.

When my fingers recall
the kiss of that ball
out at the very tip of what I was capable of—
that's when I most feel his love.

## BEYOND BLOOD

In a raffle I won Beer for a Year
and traded it for a hundred bucks
and now I sense that I have
reached the other side
of some great circle
and each transaction here
is the opposite of what it was
back where I started
trading money for beer
day in, day out
daily bread...

At Cana Jesus turned water into wine
If he'd had the disease
that runs through my family—
no, it doesn't run, it carpools—
Jesus would've gotten stuck right there
for five years, or forever.

Instead of stopping
he went on at some nameless place
to turn loaves and fishes into
a lot more loaves and fishes
a miracle he liked so much
he did it again a little later.

At Mass on Sunday morning
the bread and wine
become his body and blood
water to wine, wine to blood...
Is anything beyond blood?

Bread can mean money;
passing the basket

some see the selling of the miracle
some the collection
of the leftover bread.
Body can mean dead

Over the phone
I turned beer into bread.
Not that impressive
as miracles go:
grain and yeast, both of them
I remember the yeasty smell

of Wonder Bread baking
the North Station on Sunday night
when my father would take me
to the seven o'clock train back to school
the warm kitcheny smell of the rising bread
that Built Strong Bodies 8 Ways
the terrible sadness of Sunday night
the echoing station
the father who sent me
the long ride back
alone at 14, 15, 16, 17
no question ever
in either of our minds
that I should go
and God knows
we always tried
to do the thing we should

I don't remember
the last time I saw him
before the pre-dawn phone call
it must have been
one of those Sunday nights
over forty years
and only now do I notice
that I never stopped to remember

the last time
never stopped to ask myself what was
the last thing that he said to me
maybe it was 'I hear them honking for me'

maybe it was 'don't look back'
that's how I live
I must have got it someplace

The bells of Sunday morning signified
be still, the holy part is coming
The bells of Sunday evening said
be quick, the train's about to go

Homework taken out of overnight bag
ignored in favor of staring
out into darkness
not looking back
but not ahead either;
laterally
looking for a luminous fish
to rise from the moonlit surface
of some nameless pool;
hearing Dopplering bells as
the train raced through
the twisted crucifixes
of grade crossings;
looking for epiphany
from the lighted window
of some trackside house;
looking for signs and wonders;
thinking I was the one
bound for the underworld.

Oh that I could
from this side of the circle
tell that sad sweet boy
there *is* a transformation
but it is long and slow
and with or without your consent
the gift your father
lays upon the altar
is your whole self
the stuff of miracle.

## I Didn't Miss the Robins

till we were down the Cape that weekend
and there they were again
on the grassy banks that line the highway;
on lawns, resolute among the blowing leaves,
intent on sound beneath the surface;
thronging the branches of small trees
with yellowed leaves and bright red berries
where they arrive singly
but always seem to depart
in furious one-on-one pursuit,
a feeding and mating frenzy like—
well, a lot like *summer* on the Cape.

The first robin of spring
is like the clicking of a tumbler
in some marvelously complex lock,
a milestone like a birthday,
the longest day of the year,
the first time I told my father
that I loved him.

But there's never anything about
the last robin of fall
that announces it
as last.

## CAREFUL WHAT YOU ASK FOR

I was just old enough
to be out on the sidewalk by myself,
and every day I would come home crying,
beaten up by the same little girl.

I was Jackie, the firstborn,
the apple of every eye,
gratuitous meanness bewildered me,
and as soon as she'd hit me,
I'd bawl like a baby.

I knew that boys were not supposed to cry,
but they weren't supposed to hit girls either,
and I was shocked when my father said,
"Hit her back."

I thought it was a great idea,
but the only thing I remember
about that girl today
is the look that came over her face
after I *did* hit her back.

She didn't cry; instead
her eyes got narrow and I thought,
"Jackie, you just made a *terrible* mistake,"
and she really beat the crap out of me.
It was years before I trusted my father's advice again.

I eventually learned to fight—
enough to protect myself—
from girls—
but the real issue was the crying,
and that hasn't gone away.

Oh, I don't cry any more,
I don't sob, I don't make noise,
I just have hairtrigger tearducts, and always
at all the wrong things: supermarket openings;
Tom Bodett saying, "We'll leave the light on for ya."

In movies I despise the easy manipulation
that never even bothers to engage my feelings,
it just comes straight for my eyes,
but there's not a damn thing I can do about it,
and I hate myself for it.

The surreptitious noseblow a discreet
four minutes after the operative scene;
my daughters are on to me, my wife;
they all know *exactly* when to give me that quick,
sidelong glance. What must they think of me?

In real life I don't cry any more
when things hurt. Never a tear at seventeen
when my mother died, my father.
I never cried for my first marriage.

But today I often cry when things turn out well:
an unexpected act of simple human decency;
new evidence, against all odds,
of how much someone loves me.

I think all this is why I never wanted a son.
I always supposed my son would be like me,
and that when he'd cry it would bring back
every indelible humiliation of my own life,

and in some word or gesture
I'd betray what I was feeling,
and he'd mistake, and think I was ashamed of him.
He'd carry that the rest of his life.

Daughters are easy: you pick them up,
you hug them, you say, "There there.
It's all right. Everything is going to be
*all right*." And for that moment you really
believe that you can make enough of it right

enough. The unskilled labor of love.
And if you cry a little with them for all
the inevitable gratuitous meannesses of life,
that crying is not to be ashamed of.

But for years my great fear was the moment
I might have to deal with a crying son.
But I don't have one.
We came close once, between Megan and Kathleen;
the doctors warned us there was something wrong,

and when Joan went into labor they said
the baby would be born dead.
But he wasn't: very briefly,
before he died, I heard him cry.

## HARD TIMES & EASY CHAIRS

In the pattern of the chair, the roofs are worn
away in places from the houses. Bought
when we were married, nice enough; later on
we'd buy the really good stuff—so we thought.
The first two years the chair belonged to me,
claimed by my stains, the heap of my debris.

Daughters began to come. I know that this
was not your wily plan, to get Jack's chair;
sitting was never your idea of bliss,
and life is not, in its allotments, fair.
Whatever. A step table dislodged my pile.
It held an ashtray, book, your coffee cup
and rosary. Thus prepared to stay awhile,
you'd settle down to nurse our child. And up
the scale of useful things rose my old chair,
become a place of nurture, place of prayer.

Megan, Kathleen, Avenging Annie, each
as plump and ruddy, sweating at your breast,
as you are slim, pale, cool. Eyes close, hands reach
as though to sift the air. They come to rest,
by seeming chance, on you, and satisfied,
they settle, flex, and then relax. Who would
not be content? If objects could take pride,
swagger, like me when I do something good,
like getting paid, then there would be no living
with this chair, shabby scene of so much giving.

Most things don't fall apart; they show the wear,
and we abandon them. So with the chair.
We have worn too, but in the wear we've grown—
by gift unearned, unasked, against our wishes;
as each night, after supper, when you've gone
to sit and nurse a child, I wash the dishes.

# CONFESSIONAL POEM

*(so titled to distinguish it
from all my other poems)*

Clinging to driftwood, caught in
a backwater of the stream that runs between
Tradition and What's Happenin' Now,
we were the rearguard of the last generation
of Catholics who put church ahead
of birth control. Crisis of conscience
when one of us broke rank,
paddled to the further bank,
went to a clinic and got The Pill.
But with this caveat: don't start

till after your next period.
Too late. God's will.
For some of us that first child meant
that we would never own a house,
that we had lost the one slim chance
we'd ever have to pass Go,
get on the good side of the curve.
The little curragh we were equipped to build
rode gunwale-deep just carrying two.
The old country song:

"Every time we get ahead, it's got
another mouth to feed…." Compromises
of the seventies, trying to ride loyalty,
but not all the way to self-immolation.
The Rhythm Method was worth at least one baby.
Papal Roulette. We had virtues, but rhythm
wasn't one of them. Some tried to minimize
the commitment to sin by using condoms during
fertile periods only, but that was like
predicting weather: January's cold

and June is warm, but in March it's hard to know
where the rain will fall, and where the snow.
And repression generates enormous energy. Tell us
we can't have sex and it's all we can think about.
Try not to have a baby and she's late if your eye lingers
on her underpants on the clothesline, if your fingers
long to stroke even that little stretch of flesh
that's no longer shoulder, but not yet breast.
No electricity without dams. We were the dammed.
Power was the one thing there was always enough of.

And always that one indomitable salmon sperm
resolved to fight his way upstream, ovum or bust.
In the end we found it too hard to believe
in a powerplant micromanager god vengeful
over which floodgate was released, what orifice
an organ emptied into, how either might be
sheathed for the encounter. By private ballot
in crucifix-hung bedrooms we voted for a god
of larger vision. The dam let go and much
was washed away—like confession. What the Church

didn't know wouldn't trigger Inquisition.
But that decision was still one child ahead,
while still we connived in vain
to have it both ways. Husbands froze
when wives said, "Guess what?" But we had time
to get used to the idea, get a room ready.
Catholic family planning took nine months.
There were no unwanted children; we just
never had the particular joy of wanted ones.
The whole conception was alien to us.

Miscarriages were whirlpools.
We consoled each other, thought we were okay,
but something was gone out of us,
heart for the white water still to come,
some filament of courage

15

that would not be missed till later,
the way you don't notice a child growing
unless you're not there for a time
or the child isn't.
We felt that we had failed, and would again.

We felt all feelings any parents feel
who lose a child. And one additional, that
had we put it into words they would have been,
"I don't know how we could have stayed afloat."
Sometimes I miss confession, miss
the expression of contrition.
Bless me, father, for I have sinned.
The baby went over the side and died,
and tangled up with all the grief,
I felt relief.

## LET THE CHILDREN BOOGIE

Friday nights, bathing suit under her clothes,
dry underwear and towel in a plastic shopping bag,
every movement, every stillness speaking
excitement barely contained, Kathleen's dad
would bring her to the Murphy Pool for open swim.
He'd drop her off at the women's locker room,
then rush to change so he could be in the water
at the shallow end when she came
through the door into the pool.
Her eyes would search, he'd wave,
and she'd break into a unique gait—
not running, running wasn't allowed
at the Murphy Pool, everyone knew that—

but not walking either,
some unique form of ambulation,
with a lot of hip,
heels never touching wet tile floor—
or maybe not unique, maybe just natural
to a very short, compact person,
barefoot and tremendously excited,
picking the quickest way
across a great slipperiness
through a swarm of hyperactive kids,
none of whom was actually running.
Quite.

How many packed the little pool those nights?
How many heads bobbed above the waves
shrieking to their friends?
one hundred? two?
How many bare feet pattered
on the margins impelled by
a welter of conflicting
interpenetrating motivations

like a street scene in a Zeffirelli film,
he the only adult—

except for the harried lifeguard,
whistle never far from his lips
in the terrible tension
of authority figures everywhere
who think, "If they turn on me,
they'll tear me to pieces."
Kathleen's dad said a silent prayer for him,
knowing that if the lifeguard went,
he was next.

Kathleen would search out dry surface for her bag,
then come to the edge and kneel and dip her hand
and stand, squeeze shut her eyes, lean forward
and jump toward him, one knee slightly raised,
arms outstretched, ready to wrap
around his shoulders. And from that moment
they were in the water pretty much
until eight-thirty

unless the lifeguard blew his whistle
and ordered everyone to sit down and be silent;
lifeguards get a sixth sense
the first time they put white stuff on their nose
they can smell bad things about to happen...

Kathleen's dad would make her do exercises,
pushing off the wall and gliding to him.
Each week another six inches, and she'd complain
but he'd be stern, and she
would understand this was the price,
that she should learn her own buoyancy,
the marvelous tendency of humans
to rise to surface....

But mostly there was bobbing.
Out just deep enough that he could still
touch bottom with his legs extended.
He'd bend and unbend his knees,
bob up and down, she using him
loosely for support but keeping
her own head above water—
up, down, up, relaxed, hypnotic
like some sea creature large and still
that waits camouflaged
for things to come to it

while the clock crept interminably
toward eight-thirty
and the noise—the screams of girls
outraged by boys, boys outraged
by other boys, little kids
outraged by big kids
and crying to the lifeguard,
kids yelling across the pool to friends,
kids explaining why it might
have *looked* like they were running—
kids yelling for the sake of yelling
because they were kids
and it was Friday night
and a single shouted syllable
would ricochet to Monday morning
before it petered out.
Sooner or later, every week,
as they bounced up and down,
Kathleen's dad would start to sing.

Always the same thing,
a misremembered fragment
of the chorus of a David Bowie song:
"Let the children boogie,
Let the children boogie,
Let all the children boogie."

At the first notes,
Kathleen would look around
to see if some wise child
was noticing this eccentric man,
connecting him to her,
and out of the embarrassment of all
children in all times over the inexplicable
behavior of parents she'd say, "Daddy,
please don't sing."

And every week he would reply,
"Kathleen, Daddy *has* to sing."

And she would accept that this, too,
was part of the price.
Maybe she understood
that this was *necessary* eccentricity,
that his sanity was something needed
all the support it could get.

She wouldn't object
when he resumed:
"Let the children boogie,
Let the children boogie,
Oh let the children boogie."

Sometimes we set out to teach one thing,
and we end up teaching something else.
All those years ago.
Kathleen's grown up
into quite the young woman.
She's a pretty good swimmer—
but Lord, she loves to boogie.

## BADLANDS

The little Chevy Spectrum
with Springsteen blasting
swings into the Sunoco station
just off the Southeast Expressway
late on a Saturday afternoon
at the end of a long August heat wave
A nondescript man in cutoffs
gets stiffly out at the pump marked SELF
while the car rocks and squeaks where it stands
he reads the pump directions intently
before pumping the second-best octane

Suddenly the other three doors open
and in what looks for a second like a jailbreak
four girls in sneakers shorts and tee-shirts
bounce out of the car and into their teen years
one of them belting out Badlands along with Bruce
and the four of them start to rock'n'roll
on the oilsoaked tarmac

Passing cars honk
the man finishes filling the tank
goes inside to pay 11.86
the girls are now into linked arms and high kicks
all the unconscious grace that so amazes males
one of them has long, long legs
the singer now is bellowing
deep infectious rolling belly-laughs

The man comes back to the car
smiles a little Okay let's go
squeezes into the driver's seat
the four girls scramble quickly in
like sparrows on a danger signal
or Bell's Theorem particles
the singer riding shotgun
the little car accelerates out into the rotary
and despite fourteen cents change
two attendants stand and applaud
because

*the highway's jammed with broken heroes...*
*till these badlands*
*start treating*
*us good*

# THE FAITHFUL MEN

*in memoriam Charles Purrelli*

The faithful men who go to work each day,
raise families on the pittances they make,
realize, like swimmers tiring halfway
across a wider than it looked like lake,
that this is serious, people depend,
some very small, upon them to maintain
their stroke. Strangers speed by in boats and send
up waves to buffet them. "They're very game,
these swimmer chaps," they nod to one another.
"They like a little chop." But they are not
dismayed, the faithful men: they have their second
wind. As though expected, they are being beckoned;
something unseen moves with them on the water,
and from the shore, unlooked-for, calls a brother.

## SHELVES

One whole day my college roommate Hobson
walked around chanting a phone number to
himself. At seven o'clock that night he
would need it on the tip of his tongue, and
no mistake.

          Seven came and it all went
smoothly. But later that same night, Hobson
went to call his lifelong home and could not
remember the number there. Our other
roommate, Spring (premed), said, "Bill, you see what
this implies. From now on everything
you learn will force out something the same size,
and it's absolutely random. If I
were you I think I'd do some soul-searching
before continuing my education.
Even one music class—you might never
make it back to the room. If that happens
(God forbid), can I have your stuff? Would you
mind writing something, now, to that effect?"

Maybe it really works something like that.
Why is it we can remember the names
of the kids in our third grade class? I think
it's because we were just starting to stock
the cavernous warehouse of memory,
and we knew no better than to fill the front
shelves first, and with whatever came to hand.

I ran this theory by my wife and she
said her stuff never makes it to the shelves;
her stuff is all in boxes, on the floor.

At a family wake a while back I
was astonished to see my Uncle Mike,
my grandfather's brother. I had thought he

24

was dead years ago. His son told me he
didn't know what day it was, he never
did any more—but why did he need to?
It had to be painstakingly explained
to Mike who I was, but once he had me
placed in his lattice of recallable
relationships, I was able to sit
with him and pick his brain of treasures that
I had believed irretrievably lost.

He played third base and shortstop, just like me.
Graduated from Boston Latin, like
my daughters. He remembers the first time
he saw my grandmother: she was wearing
a raccoon coat and he thought, "That's the best
looking woman I've ever seen." Gramma?

He says the best job he ever had was
managing an office in City Hall,
where he booked the occasional wager
on the side—he makes it sound like it was
part of the job description. He can still
recall the number of the bookie in
the North End he would phone his bets in to.

I made a date to sit with Uncle Mike
again; next time I'll bring a notebook and
a tape deck, to rescue the old stories.
For myself, for my daughters—someday for
their kids, maybe.

                    What kind of ballplayer
was my grandfather? Did my great-grandfather
have a temper that got him in trouble?
Did he love his children, and did he let
them know it? Have the McCarthy women
always been strong? the men good-looking?

25

I know that every time I visit Mike,
I'll have to step him painstakingly
to who I am. The shelves of his memory
are full, the contents irreplaceable.
They should not make way for things unneeded,
obvious, or self-explanatory.

# THE MOON & JUSTIN O'SHEA

*for my daughter Annie, who
has dodged some serious bullets*

I could sense the rising
of the temper he was known for.
"It moves when I move," he insisted.
I tried to show it moved with me too,

but he observed that no, it didn't,
I could walk as far as I wanted
and the moon wouldn't budge an inch
as long as he stayed put.

I stabbed half-hearted at explaining
it was *relative*,
it only *seemed* that way,
and it seemed that way to

every body that moved,
but he was seven
and I was just eight
and I didn't understand it

nearly well enough myself
to convert an infidel
all caught up in the passion of discovery
that the biggest thing in the heavens

cared whether he put one foot
in front of the other—and really,
is that so fantastic?
Adults have believed for centuries

astrology, and Justin O'Shea
had the evidence of
his own eyes to prove
exactly that connectedness.

I gave it one more try
but of course it was no good my taking
six steps—really big steps this time—
down Saxton Street and bearing witness

to the shifting of the moon across
the roofs of three-deckers while Justin
rooted to the sidewalk and for him
that ghostly blue-white sphere stood

arrested in its flight
across the bright blue skies,
no test I could devise
did not add fuel to his fanatic fire.

And tonight, on the flight home from New York,
I'm gazing out the rightside window
at Long Island Sound
and at the long straight silver

reflection of the pale round full moon
itself reflecting light from somewhere else
light bouncing every whichway
around the solar system

and I still don't understand, quite,
why the line of moon upon the water
should seem to follow this plane
and no other, you'd think water

would simply glow wherever moonlight
struck with no regard to whether
one particular traveler happened to be
looking out his assigned window…

the effect especially striking as we
come in over the Connecticut coast
dark stretches turn out to conceal
networks of inlets that are invisible until

the reflection catches them and they
switch on silver and dart zigzag
in every direction at once like
rivers of mercury escaping

from a broken fever thermometer
like a hasty Etch-a-Sketch
that erases behind itself as it goes
like Annie's conversation.

And I think about the day just passed
with my once-more resurrected daughter,
pale visions of quicksilver reflections
of my own neglected dreams.

I even went to the museum with her
and played the fool all day
(a talent that I have).
She asked me what I wanted

to see and I said,
"The biggest thing in the museum."
and she laughed, she laughed at
every silly thing I said.

But the biggest thing in the museum
*was* Annie; she moved with me.
Justin was right:
heaven does care.

# THE ORTHOPOD

I finally had my appointment with the orthopod,
and he arranged for x-rays, eventually announced
there were a lot of miles left in these old hips,
but that jogging was going through them like
the Prodigal Son, buying rounds for the gentile house
in some other god's country.

He said although the x-rays were not good,
they weren't as bad as my range of motion
had led him to expect.
This told him there'd been tightening
in the soft tissue, from disuse.

It's a natural consequence of small pain:
it starts to hurt to cross our legs,
so we stop doing it,
and all that muscle, tendon, cartilage, ligament,
just tightens up that much more.

As in a marriage: you get a sharp answer
when you get home and ask,
"Is there time for a run before supper?"
and you could have asked
"How was your day?" but there wasn't time
for both, there never is, you have to choose—
and once that line's been drawn
you don't want to make concessions,
so though you don't step across the line
you make a big loop around it,
you start running home from work instead—
a six-mile run, in traffic,
through the ugliest parts of Boston—
but the question no longer comes up,
and when you do get home,
there is time, and you can say,
smugly, "How was your day."

And in the soft tissue of the marriage,
from disuse, tightness builds.
Parts that were elastic petrify;
places that were lubricated dry.

I asked this orthopod if he were me,
would he stop jogging today?
and he said, "No, it's an addiction
and you have your mental state
to think about too."

George Sheehan, the Running Doctor,
was speaking once about how running helps
people coming off addictions. Someone asked,
"Isn't running itself just one more addiction?"
"For some of us," the Running Doctor said,
"addiction may be the only viable way of life."

My young friend Brian Comiskey tells me
not to listen to the orthopod.
He quotes Nietzche to me:
"Whatever doesn't kill me makes me stronger."
Right, Brian, you know a great line when you hear one;
but Nietzche is dead, isn't he?
Brian observes, "So is the Running Doctor."
Touché.

It's been a tough year,
one injury after another serving notice
that although maybe man was made to run in packs,
barefoot, out on the Serengeti plain,
carrying clubs and sharp sticks
and fanning out to form a loop around some edgy prey,
a wildebeest, perhaps, or maybe zebra—
sometimes, on the really good days, I could feel that,
that this was what I *evolved* to do—
still, sedentary life and concrete sidewalks
take their toll.

And maybe even on the Serengeti,
fourteen years was a good run for your money.

So one more for old time sake
and then cold turkey.
I always heeded Satchel Paige:
"Never look back;
somethin might be gainin on you."

## LEFT BRAIN / RIGHT BRAIN

Through the day
never more than half awake.
Almost afraid that it would always be like this.
Not caring quite enough actually to be afraid.

Oh yes Jack you will do Great Things.
I'd smile and nod and think Perhaps—
or maybe ordinary things
with great absence of effort.

Like that. Then go to...
Ah.
There it is.
It's all right now.
Warm liquid grace filtering down through me,
runneling among the frozen places,
magical— I turn a little on my stool,
just a little, just a hair. Oh, I am in control,
in perfect, absolute control...

If God were to put a piano in front of me in this instant,
I'd reach out my right hand,
extend my finger with majestic delicacy;
the note that I would strike
would be unutterably perfect,
the Jericho note, only purer, more compelling.
The world had never heard a note
like I would strike...

Or a woman.
Had there been a woman there,
then there would be secret words
that would unlock a woman.
In this instant, I would have those words,
that Jericho phrase...
I'd pause a little,

make her wonder Will he say it?
Please God make him say it.
I would own her I would *OWN* her.
And then I'd say it,
my voice low, intimate and clear,
so that her very bowels would quiver,
and liquid warmth would curl upward inside her,
like incense spiraling from an altar,
following all her soft places up,
a lazy cat-stretch of a slickening message
from her vulva to her mind.
And I'd extend my finger, as if to say
You are not worthy, that I should enter you;
but what the hell...
if there had been a woman there.

And even in the midst of this omnipotence,
already half my mind connived,
When can I get drunk again?

There was no woman there. And no piano.
And had there been, and I had struck
that note to make all other notes
unnecessary and presumptuous,
the world would not have missed a beat
of conversation, not acknowledged me,
as if my note and I had never been.

What the *FUCK* do you have to do
to get the world's attention?

II.

Years later now and making love with you.
What is involved? The usual things.
Some lips, a lot of tongue—
Shall we then have the Naming of Parts?
Oh I think not. There are Activities:

34

caressing, inserting, plinking, fondling,
licking, sucking, kissing;
appreciating.
Celebrating.
I had those nipples fifty years,
and never knew that they were wired like that.
How did God ever think of this,
who lived so long alone—
but of course that must be it.

You are the blonde and tawny stuff of every daydream.
Want to try this?
        Like this?
How about this?
        Like this?

Stuff of every adolescent masturbation fantasy.
I tried SO hard not to do it. There were
times I wished that I could cut my cock off.
I made love to pictures then, pretending
I was with a real woman, believing I sinned.
Now you are real and here, yet oftentimes
my thoughts are of those magazines and playing cards
that now, Jack, you are the man in the pictures,
that other naked body,
the one that you ignored,
look closer now, the hard one, it is you,
the unremembered face, it is your own...

Ah.
There it is.
It's all right now.
This makes all those things all right.
Because
        they
                made
                        this
                                happen.

I'm sorry that I suffered,
yet I am glad I tried.

And even in the midst of this,
this benediction on a yearning lifetime,
even as I forget about you
and go rocketing into orbit on my own,
half my mind is grappling with—
                              —fear—
the fragility of the chain of events that got us here—
We could have missed…
        *We could have missed…*
                *We could have missed…*
*Aahhhhhhh.*
Ah.

Oh
    I
        have
            done
                great
                    things.

# THE SWAN ON NUTTING LAKE

*for Thomas Lux*

Among the geese and ducks
on Nutting Lake this spring,
a single swan appeared,
southwest of where
the Middlesex Turnpike
bisects the lake.
I look for him each day
as I roll through on my way
to work, from work.

He frequents the little island
in the southmost corner,
but sometimes my eye's betrayed
by a white plastic K-Mart lawn chair
sitting on a dock on the western shore
not far away from the liquor store.

I keep hoping to see a second swan,
and I bet our singleton is thinking
the same thing, scanning the sky
for some foxy female
happening to overfly
look down, spot him and think,
hey, that stud's got
a lake of his own;
and her biological clock will sound
a shrieking Mayday alarm
and all her nesting hormones
will seize control
bringing her around and down
in a long slow gliding arc

but   it   hasn't happened yet.
And more and more often lately

our singleton is turning up
in the area of that
windswept lawn chair,
so that I begin to wonder if his eye might
betray him the same way mine does me,
if that peripheral flash of white
says Swan to him too
but he *likes* that white lie,
the way that solitary men
find comfort sometimes
in airbrushed images of women.

And why am I so certain
it's a male waiting for a female anyway?
Why not female? or gay? or bi?
I guess because I
populate its head
with foolish masculine fantasies.
Thomas Lux has a poem about a guy
who hung upside down
from a bridge over a highway
to paint a message of love
for his sweetheart
only to perpetrate a particularly
gruesome misspelling
of a critical word.
After a reading someone asked why
he was so sure
the painter was male
and it's not often words fail
Lux, but on this occasion
all he could say was,

"You've *got* to be kidding."
Point being that the right to make
a public and spectacular fool of oneself
over a potential mate

is a deeply cherished
*masculine* prerogative.

So if our swan isn't a young male,
must be he's an old one.
They say swans mate for life—
though as for that I was watching
PBS about coyotes
and they said *they* mate for life
but later on they showed
this renegade young male
attempting to scale
the hindquarters of the alpha female
and I couldn't help noticing she
wasn't particularly desperate to get away....
Maybe animals mating for life
isn't a rule, exactly,
it's more like ...a *guideline*,
they're not fanatics about it.

(Actually, I wasn't really
*watching* that show,
my wife was and I
just happened to be going by.
That would be my
second wife, Alpha Carol.)

But getting back to our swan,
(now that we've established it's a he)
maybe he hasn't come
to Nutting Lake
to await a mate at all,
maybe he's come to die—

much the way that I felt after my
first marriage broke up when I
said to Grandmother Read,
"My life is very exciting

I'm doing lots of interesting things
there are terrific women at meetings
but part of me can't help feeling
that my life is over."
And she answered,
"A chapter of your life
*is* over.
The next chapter
hasn't started yet."

And I guess that's what
I'd like to say to our swan.
Bide your time, shining brother.
Keep putting one webbed foot
in front of the other.
Find solace in your solitude.
And mark the day
when you hear yourself say,
"Hey, this ain't bad.
I eat when I'm hungry
I drink when I'm dry
and if moonshine don't kill me
I'll live till I die"

Because then
you'll know you're ready
for some female swan
foxy and real to overfly
Nutting Lake and wheel
about in a long slow gliding
arc when she spots you.

No swan is an island;
don't drive her away.
Guidelines are okay,
but there's no percentage
in fanaticism.
You've lake to share;

don't settle for the company
of geese and ducks,
a plastic K-Mart lawn chair.
Remember Thomas Lux;
remember the immortal words
of Dustin Hoffman: "K-Mart sucks."

# Neponset Circle

*for my wife Carol,*
*the woman who drives me to Poetry*

The Quincy AA Group
liked to let Charlie drive
on their commitments.
He was a careful driver
who stayed a mile or two under the speed limit,
and he liked to leave a little earlier than other people would.
But he never missed a turn or had to ask for directions,
and he always got the group to the meeting
on time.

Sometimes a newcomer would ask
why they had gone from Quincy to Brockton
by way of Neponset Circle—
there are back roads into Brockton, short cuts.
An old-timer would whisper, "*Shhhh.*
*We know that there are quicker ways.*
*But Charlie likes to drive.*
*And he can get us anywhere in the world—*
*as long as he starts from Neponset Circle.*"

Most of us see the world as spiderweb,
all sorts of intricate connections,
alternate routes. A good sense of direction
and a roadmap and we'll always find our way.
Charlie saw the world as a bicycle tire,
spokes crossing each other here and there,
but all of them running straight to and from
one heart.

Over the years a lot of people got
too impatient to put up with Charlie's ways—
he wouldn't even take the Squantum Street cutoff,
they'd complain, and you could almost

*see* Neponset Circle from both ends.
Sometimes they'd maneuver themselves
into the front seat to make suggestions:
"Charlie, this right goes straight to Hancock Street."
"Yup, I know," he'd reply, and cruise right by,
while the oldtimers puffed serenely in the back.

"Insane," the dissidents called Charlie,
or "anal," if they'd had Psych 101;
"compulsive." As though we all weren't.
But he drove *them* crazy. Eventually
they'd take their own cars, thank you,
trust their own internal compasses.

And for awhile, they would look good.
They'd leave a little later and be
sipping coffee smugly when Charlie's cadre
of newcomers and oldtimers sauntered in.
But sooner or later they'd miss a turn and get lost
and a commitment would go by the boards, unmet,
and if it was a prison or a hospital,
there'd be no meeting there at all that night
and that was serious.

The oldtimers knew that it would happen
because all the alternate routers had to go on
was their own sense of direction.
Charlie had Neponset Circle.
Carol, my love,
you're *my* Neponset Circle.

# CARTALK: A LOVE POEM

The cars I drive
don't look like much I will admit,
but mostly they've got engines that won't quit
this side of a nuclear explosion.

The Shitbox Mystique: when new friends
point at dents, concerned, and ask,
"What happened to your car?" I answer,
"It was like that
when I *bought* it."

When I met Carol she was driving
a pretty good car,
except for the air-conditioner,
which used to make the engine overheat.
Carol also brought into my life
her son Seth and her mechanic, Peter—
that's another feature
of the Mystique, your mechanic
becomes part of your family,
we see more of Peter than we do of Seth,
we invited him to our *wedding*—
though I'll admit, Peter wasn't actually
*in* the wedding, and Seth was.

Now Carol likes nice things,
but what with college bills and all,
a couple years with me
and her blue Subaru
went downhill fast
and I got to see a new
side of her, that her idea of a good day
is breaking down outside a gas
station.

Eventually her engine started
overheating even without
the air-conditioner; in fact
the only way to keep the temperature
out of the red zone on a hot day
was to turn the heat *on*.
I don't think Carol's mother
ever really bought
the unlikely physics of that;
I think she thought we were
trying to make her and Ed
go home to California.

When you've got
two people driving shitboxes
you get to make some interesting decisions—
like which one to take to Connecticut.
One has no windshield fluid
because the plastic thing leaks
and Peter hasn't been able to find
a used one that fits;
the other has something *really scary*
going on with steering…
but we take it anyway,
because on the map
the road to Connecticut
looks pretty straight.

Sometimes I get home from work
and Carol's ecstatic.
"Jack, I met the most wonderful
towtruck driver today. We towed
the car to Peter's,
and he brought me back
all the way to the door.
We had the most incredible conversation!
He's a very unusual person."

Right, Carol; like you're *not*.
A couple years with me she's on
a firstname basis with every
towtruck driver in Middlesex County.
Triple-A has *us* on speed-dial.

One time we were driving
somewhere together and she reflected,
"You know, if your first marriage
had worked out better, you
wouldn't have been available
for me. And vice versa."

I thought what a classic she is,
the miles look good on her.
But both of us came as is,
with dented fenders, and random
detritus in the trunk, and I said,
"It's as if we both broke down
outside the same gas station
at the same time."

And she smiled
and then she laughed,
and then we both laughed,
a long soft asynchronous laugh
like the ticking of an engine it will take
a nuclear blast
to stop.

## CARTALK II: CATHOLICS & CARTHIEVES

I got out and walked around
to get something out of the passenger side
and the doorhandle came off in my hand.

Things happen with old cars—
but this is serious, because
the key doesn't work in the driverside,
and we'd already grown accustomed
to entering by the passenger door,
reaching across to unlock the driver's door,
then getting out and walking around—
and we don't hold that against the car:
if there's one thing we Catholics understand,
it's forgiveness.

But now we have to worry about that carthief
whose eccentricity is that he
lights up when he lays eyes on
a twelve-year-old Plymouth Horizon,
and who, although he balks
at entering cars with locks,
nonetheless knows how to hotwire one
that starts reluctantly
even when you *have* the key
and have *somehow* achieved the driverseat.

We're going to have to leave a door unlocked,
and the obvious choice would be
the driver's door, but to me that seems
too blatant an occasion of temptation.
No, I think the unlocked one should be

the *rear* door on the *passenger* side.
That way our crackpot crook would have to
enter there, reach forward to release
the passengerside front door,

get out, get in again,
reach across to unlock the driver's door,
then get out and walk around,
all this before he gets to strip
even one frayed wire.

Somewhere in that process,
even the most confirmed criminal might pause
to cross-examine his conscience
and ask the existential question:
"*Why?*
Why am I doing this?
Why do I even *want* this car?
For quick getaways? I don't think so!"

Once he starts asking questions,
anything can happen, miracles can happen,
because if there's one thing we Catholics understand,
it's redemption.

He might see Saint Christopher
watching over him from the dashboard
and think about how clean
he used to feel at thirteen
walking out of confession
late on a Saturday afternoon in fall
and wonder where it all
went wrong.

He might see my wife's picture and recall
the beautiful girl he loved when he was seventeen—
he was so sure she wanted him to call,
but certain that if he did,
she'd break his heart.

He might say what the hell,
borrow a quarter from the well
between the seats, back out

and make his way to a payphone
and try that well-remembered number,
and she might cry into the phone
and sigh, "*I've waited so long...*"

and this time she will go out with him,
and this time,
this time she will *break*
*his larcenous goddamned heart*
*and he'll* **kill** *himself*
*and burn in hell*
*for all eternity because*
if there's one thing we Catholics understand,

***it's hell.***

## CARTALK IV: THE DRIVER CARD

I came around there where the road
curved right, and pulled over to park
for my Friday night AA meeting
and this kid who'd been tailgating me
in a sharp roadster was caught
offguard and had to swerve hard
to avoid rear-ending me.

He pulled alongside and yelled,
"Why the hell didn't you signal?"
I must have been pretty mellow:
I lied my blinker'd died that day.
Unpacified, he glared contempt
and added, "Why don't you get
a *decent* car?"

I turned and regarded
the one thing in my ownership
that wasn't sitting in my furnished room,
an old Chevy Nova that my first wife
let me keep over the divorce
presumably because I was
the one who went to work.

This time I saw through that kid's eyes:
duct tape and coathanger antenna,
the unattended dents of unreported accidents,
missing hubcaps, places rusted through,
places where the paint had
flaked away and I had touched up
in a mismatched shade of blue.

Sure, I could have dispatched that kid
with some sad, wise coup or other—
like, "If you have to ask the question,
you'd never understand the answer."

Instead I thought about my mother, dead
thirty years: till we made it out of Southie
she never even had a license to drive

but when the old Buick Super had to
pass inspection she slid herself under it
and contrived a muffler out of
dish towels and dogfood cans,
and for a little while in Hingham,
horsepower smelled like horsemeat.
Her makeshift muffler quieted the car

but would have ignited it
within another mile
the awestruck inspector told her.
Dish towels:
what a woman!
When that young guy asked why
I didn't get a better car,

maybe all I had to say was,
"Son, you might as well
get used to it, because
there'll never be
enough to go around.
And always someone willing
to drive it into the ground

and then get out and walk
the rest of the way."
At the end of Good Will Hunting,
Will heads out the Pike from Southie
in that shitbox that his friends
have stitched together for him,
and you and I know

that bucket of junk
will be lucky to make

fucking Uxbridge, let alone Palo Alto.
And even if he makes it to California on foot,
you know that relationship
has about as much chance
as a quick-pick powerball ticket

neglected in the pocket
of a pair of pants
forgotten in the bottom of a closet,
because like me, Will's damaged goods,
he's packing too much baggage.
But you just might be wrong
because on that left coast there waits

(played by—as fate would dictate—
Minnie *Driver*) a woman who'll contrive
to do whatever it takes to make things work.
Whatever it takes.
And as long as that driver card is in the deck,
there is always,
*always* a chance.

# THOMAS MERTON

*for Bill McGrane*

When I was a freshman at Archbishop Williams,
my homeroom teacher was Sister Mary Josephine.
Yes, she did fit a lot of the stereotypes:
she could be waspish, she played favorites.

Sister had a huge resentment against
the Reformation, but I don't remember
her mentioning the Inquisition.
She read us terrifying stories
about tortured martyrs

and occasionally indulged
in the pedantic pleasure of a good,
satisfying, sweeping generalization.
She once told us that if a girl would smoke,
she'd drink, and if she'd drink,
she'd do anything.

I looked around the room and
a lot of boys were writing that down.
I didn't, because I knew intuitively
that I'd never forget it,
and I seem to have been right.

Looking back I've often wondered
how she could have *not* known
how helpful that information,
if true, could be to boys who
were beginning to be damned curious

about these Temptations of the Flesh
we kept hearing about.

But Sister also had a great sense of humor,
and a playful side.
She'd entered the convent as a teenager,
and maybe some teenage parts of her
came down to us miraculously unaltered,
like a pre-Cambrian butterfly
preserved in amber.

She told one story about a nun friend of hers
who had visited the Trappist monastery in Kentucky
where Thomas Merton was in residence
under the vow of silence.

Her friend saw one of the monks,
passing in his cassock through the parking lot,
admiring a big, shiny, late-model car.
Then he stuck out his hand and ran
his fingertips along the hood,
luxuriating in the unnatural smoothness.

The nun reported the vision back to her sisters
and they all agreed that the monk had to be
Merton—who, before his conversion,
had admittedly given himself over
to unspecified forms of worldliness,
some of them undoubtedly better left
unspoken, but others perhaps comparatively
innocent—like an intimate appreciation
of the heady temptation
of conspicuous consumption.

Now, having told this story,
I see that I might have
misled you in my title,

that this might not be
a story about Thomas Merton at all.

But it's certainly about
Sister Mary Josephine and her friends,
and maybe about the fascination
that young girls have with rock stars,
and what that fascination might look like
trapped in amber.

I ask you to forgive the bait-and-switch,
and I firmly resolve
to continue to confess my sins
as quickly as I recognize them.

And by the way,
what Sister told us
about girls who smoke
proved to be misleading too—

although even today,
whenever I see a woman lighting up,
I still feel a stupid stab
of totally inappropriate
hope.

## OLD JOHN'S BLESSING ON
## EROTIC POETRY NIGHT

Adam was a prototype,
Eve was a work of art.
A young man seeking praise
volunteers that he has taken up
with a woman he does not find

physically attractive.
He believes she might deliver
"undiscovered wonders."
Old John draws wetly on his cold pipe,
admonishes, "Son,

God made them beautiful to us
for a reason. If you can't see
the beauty in her, get out
of her way. A woman is entitled
to someone who can."

The young man asks
(not the same day, but another day),
"When you were young like me,
and the juice was running strong,
was there any line that worked

particularly well for you?"
Old John nods. "It's passing strange,"
he says. "But every time I admitted to a girl
that I wasn't very good in bed,
but I was fun,

we would be making the beast with two backs
before the clock struck one."
The young man ponders, then suggests,
"The Cindy Lauper effect?" But Old John has
no idea who Cindy Lauper is—or    was.

A famous atheist once dismissed
the book <u>The Prophet</u> as "a book
that college students use to get laid."
Old John considers this the standard
against which all books should be measured.

Old John offers,
"Our willingness to contradict
ourselves on their behalf
is very near the heart
of what they want from us."

And, "Whenever two people lie down together
for nothing but sex,
inevitably, when they arise,
one and only one of them
is in love."

The stakes are high; many opt out
entirely. This karma keeps them
reincarnating until they learn
what the best reason is
for coming to this planet.

The young man asks,
"Have we then been talking about sex?
or about love?"
By way of answer,
Old John nods.

The young man asks,
"When is sex the best?"
Old John says,
"Now. Always now.
That is its blessing."

And all that it requires
is two people
with an utterly uncomplicated
will to please each other
and a room.

WHAT ODYSSEUS MIGHT HAVE SAID TO KALYPSO
AS THEY GAZED OUT AT DAWN THE ROSY-FINGERED
RISING UP OUT OF THE WINE-DARK SEA
IF KALYPSO HAD ACTUALLY OFFERED HIM IMMORTALITY
AS IT SEEMED FOR A FEW PAGES THAT SHE MIGHT

O mistress goddess nymph
you who dwell beyond what we call beauty
men and women live and die
in hundreds of our generations
without one glimpse of splendor
while you, your every breath is splendor
fabrics that grace your body
glow where they have touched you
like altarcloths in candlelight.

We come from nowhere
make our little rounds
wither and die and go back into nothing
while you go on
resplendent and unchanging….

Mistress goddess immortal
you have called out love
from depths in me I never knew I had
I have worshiped and cherished you.
Lover, who have lavished on me the gift
of sharing your bed of coming to know
the slick and ever slicker
inner surfaces of your body
the smell of your sex in my beard
your cadences the rhythm of
your moans when passion takes you
till they are more familiar than the beating
of this heart I used to think was mine
the far-inward look in your eyes
when our faces close together
but the point of things is elsewhere

59

the dream-state that overtakes you
sometimes when it pleases you
to pleasure me—

yours is a love that does not need to be
forever thinking ahead to the next thing
because there is after all
forever—

You are the island, we are grains of sand.
The tide rolls us in
deposits us awhile upon your strand
then at the wine-dark whim of the sea
or worse, its vast disinterest
we are swept away again to rest
forever unaccounted and unmissed
upon the ocean floor
no one ever to tell our story.

You offer me what all men dream about.
We sweat and strive, endure, connive
train our bodies school our minds
on the dream of the offchance
that now and again we might win this—
the boudoir prepared for our coming
the hero's welcome the lover's kiss.

You are the moon
that night by night is different
and month by month the same.
You show us only what you'd have us see.
We are wisps of cloud that drift
across your face by night
we cannot hold one shape
for even the brief moment
we are visible only by your light.

Maybe, in a thousand years or so
men or gods more wise and eloquent
will have devised a graceful way of saying
what you know is coming—

there is another, and I belong to her
in ways I never understood
until I learned from you
the wisdom of the heart.
Penelope: is she as beautiful as you,
as skilled at sacred arts of love?
Does she have as much to teach,
as much to offer me as you?

I will not disparage her to you
but no, on all counts.
You are a goddess
if this were a competition
like that other one
she and I would be humiliated forever
glimpsing the depths of our unworthiness.

But what it has taken
all my adventures to teach me is that
if there is a point in being human
it isn't being first or best or winning
it has not to do with competition.
My choice is not which one of you is better
my choice is simply which of you is mine.

I once told someone that my name was No-man.
Today I know that I am one man—
not less than one, nor more than man.

Maybe there is no meaning to human life
but if there is it has to do
with things begun in earnest.
It's with Penelope that I shall find it.

The life that we began was flawed,
a fragile, mortal, human thing.
Already it is dreadfully curtailed
maybe maimed beyond recovery.
I need      I need to go back
for what little may be left.

Mistress, goddess, I am at your mercy.
Do with me what you will.
Snuff out the guttering candle that I am.
Or, exalting me in legend sentence me
to some eternal torment like Prometheus.
Or humor me, and smile me back to bed
making me forget all this
like a dream that flickered dimly in the light of dawn
that I never tried to apprehend
that left behind it no more than
a child's footprint in wet sand
between wave's retreat
and wave's advance.

Or grant my wish
and send me with your blessing on my road
a road not given to anyone but me
and seal forever in the hearts of gods and men
that this is how a human being should act
and this, a god.

*In 1986, the Boston Red Sox lost the World Series in particularly*
*excruciating fashion, even for the Red Sox. The most memorable*
*play of that Series was a ground ball that went through the legs*
*of a Red Sox first baseman named Bill Buckner.*

## THE WALK OF LIFE

You weren't here that long
near the end of a career
that wasn't quite Hall of Fame.
We knew you through the box scores
and the car radio.

And I remember as that fateful season neared its end
almost hearing tears in the announcer's voice
as he tried to describe the sight of you
careering around second on your two
terribly damaged legs
stretching a double into a triple.
"Gallant" was the word he used
and gallant is how I remember you.

But we live in a time
when Nike erects a billboard
in sight of the Olympic athletes:
"*You Don't Win Silver,*
      *You Lose Gold,*"
and so it is that some remember only
the nightmare tenth inning of Game Six
the big bouncing grounder
that found a way
between those gallant legs, condemning you
to the underworld of those who made it
to within a whisker of the top,
who beat all the competition

except one.
The inmost circle of that underworld's reserved
for the Fred Merkles, and Roy Reigelses
Denny Galehouses, and Mike Dukakises
for those second-place finishers
destined to be remembered particularly
for their *hammartia*
that one error in judgment
the base untouched
the photo-op in the tank

Oh, Billy Buck,
why did it have to happen to you?

I once saw a music video
that began with a long string of clips
of athletes looking foolish—
stone-fingered tight end
juggles ball five times
before linebacker demolishes him
and ball drops harmless out of bounds;
runner trips over second base as though
surprised that it was there;
tall Caucasian butchers slam dunk,
comes away bleeding.
Then suddenly it changes—
wide receiver soars in the end zone
gets one hand on the ball
but it sticks
and he cradles it to his belly
surrendering his body to the furious crash
of the cornerback he just burned
in a moment of such violent airborne beauty
such conspicuous gallantry
that you thank God videotape exists
and you pray that long after we've destroyed ourselves
aliens will land and find this tape
and wonder at the mad grace

of such a race.
And the soundtrack sings
 *"You do the walk,*
*you do the walk of li-hi-hife..."*

I was surrounded by children
when I saw that video
my daughters and their cousins
and like someone suddenly filled with the spirit
I stood up and began to preach
the brilliance of what we were watching:
that if you want to achieve
anything spectacular in life
*you have to risk humiliation*
and this one time they all listened to me
fascinated like...
   pigeons in Assisi.

And I can still see you
standing stiff and tall,
the ball bouncing toward you big and slow
and I know you're thinking,
*"Thank God, at least we're out of the inning,"*
but then it's a little *too* slow
and the batter is tearassing down the line toward you
faster than anyone named Mookie has a right to move

so you reach deep into
the gallant center of your soul
and you will the ball to get there
   a little quicker
because now it has to
and there is one tired instant in there
when you believe that you can do this,
that you can *will* the ball there—
it's believing in yourself *too much...*

*[long sigh]*

I guess what bothers me most is our dishonesty.
We know this happens to a thousand people
one way or another every hour of every day.
But we can't live with that knowledge.
So we joke, we say,
*"Like Bill Buckner, ho ho ho"*
fostering the pretense we're too good
for this too happen to us
when what is spectacularly obvious
is we're not even close to being good enough
ever to be exposed to anything *this bad*
our errors go unnoticed
because *we* go unnoticed
      and we *like it that way....*

If we were honest, your name would be spoken
only after the lights were out
and then only between two persons
who had achieved the deepest intimacy
who knew that they could turn to one another
in the darkness
when the fear was on them
one of them might gently brush
the shoulder of the other
and the other one might
swim up from the depths of sleep and whisper
*"What is it, my darling?"*
and the one might sigh,
*"Bill Buckner,"*
and the other might
caress the one and whisper

*"Shhh.  It's all right.*
*Sleep will come,*
*when you're not looking.*
*Morning will come, and breakfast,*
*and things that should be easy*
*will be easy once more.*
*It's the Walk of Life.*
*You've walked it before*
*and you* **will** *walk it again.*
*Shhh     now        beloved."*

## The Trailer Park
## on Mount St. Helens

On the way back down it was apparent,
the first settlement we came to was
a trailer park,
which made me think how
once a week all summer

there's a picture
page three of The Globe
of some sleepy, dusty southern town
where a tornado's torn
a trailer park apart

they're magnets for tornadoes
maybe they're the breeding ground...
which set me wondering about
the kind of people that would
live in a trailer park

on Mount St. Helens, are they
the kind that when they see a tree
knocked down by lightning
park their car next to it
thinking now it should be safe?

Do they visit California
only after earthquakes?
Florida only after hurricanes?
New Jersey only after... no, there is no
good time to visit New Jersey.

Maybe they were already living in
some trailer park in Kansas
and got tired of waiting
for the tornado
then they read in their

trailer park tabloid about this
hamlet on Mount St. Helens
where every day's a roll of the dice
tornado or volcano
volcano or tornado

or real life
life in a trailer park....
And what about those tiny
wisps of color we kept seeing
against the background of the mountainside

that looked like corduroy,
the way that all the evergreens
were leveled in the same direction?
Those wisps turned out to be
            hang gliders

drifting like hawks upon the wind
that swept like the breath of God
down the valley and up
the mountainside. Are they there
in spite of the volcano?

or because of it? I once read
a doomsday novel about an asteroid
colliding with the earth
in which this surfer knows
a tidal wave is coming

and he paddles out, far out,
on his board to ride that tidal wave
and he is unsurprised
and yes satisfied
when that tsunami smashes him

against the twenty-second story
of a beachfront condo along

with all his beach-bum buddies
who went out with the same idea in mind.
Maybe those gliders read that doomsday novel,

maybe that's the ultimate ride
they're hanging around for.
My wife is nervous now about
the asteroids. Part of the reason
she moved East from California

was earthquakes, her intuition
that the west coast is a natural
disaster waiting for the least
tremor to trigger the fault.
The other part was her personal life

was the same, except for natural.
The asteroids have always been,
but now she knows they're there
it's as if she'd had a personal
collection letter from God

announcing he can crush us
any time the spirit moves.
I try to argue that the same facts
also mean God's been protecting all this time.
"And think about the flood," I say,

"the rainbow. 'God set his bow
in the sky as token of his
covenant with us that he would
never again destroy the world...
*by water.*'"

But even as I speak those unconvincing
words I come aware of all the loopholes
in *that* leaky promise, till water

doesn't seem that bad an option....
And anyway, what kind of God protects

from things he set in motion
in the first place?
And suddenly I begin to understand
why the Mafia got started
in a Catholic country,

country where gladiators used to greet
their emperor with the only legitimate thing
left to say to our trailer parkers:
"*We, who are about to die,*
            *salute you.*"

# THE POTATO PEOPLE

*(after watching the PBS series, "The Irish in America")*

When I was a kid
my mother used to make great French fries.
She'd wash the potatoes
lay them on a towel
and her hands would fly over them,
never using a peeler,
always the Good Sharp Knife.
Half the time she'd slice
a finger in the process;
she never made a big deal out of it
so we never thought twice about it.
I remember the trails of peels,
linked like paper dolls,
that went into the garbage.

My mother's French fries were
loud in the pan;
you'd have to raise your voice
to be heard over them.
They'd fry up crisp and dark brown
and we'd lavish them with salt
that would melt into them,
and inside they'd be soft and sweet.

We were all delighted
when frozen fries came out;
mum converted overnight,
maybe to save her fingers.
We could have them much more often,
and if we ever noticed
that something extraordinary
had been lost,
I suppose we chalked it up to life
being full of tradeoffs.

II

What's an Irish 7-course meal?
A sixpack and a potato.

They called us the Potato People.
Thackeray described us as
"ragged, ruined, and cheerful"
like the land.
We lived in our hillside clans,
and we loved to laugh and fight
and drink and recite
and sing and dance and procreate
and all we ever ate
was the potato.

We'd harvest our potatoes in the fall
and put enough away
to feed our family for the year.
And life was good—for
forty-four, forty-five weeks.

Somehow we always forgot
that the old potatoes
never made it through summer
without rotting.
No freezers then.
Men would take to the road,
looking for work, they'd say,
and when they'd come home
to harvest the new crop
some of the weaker children
would have been winnowed out.
Darwinian potatoes.

We must have known
the system wasn't designed
with us in mind;

but life is full of tradeoffs,
and hey, we didn't make the world.
And maybe it always seemed that
someday, it just might work.
And if it ever did,
we'd have it all then,

without change and without
            compromise.

III

My personal search for the perfect potato
persists. Here and there
I've thought for awhile
that I'd found it:
my first taste of shoestring potatoes
at the Universe Diner
on Route 66 in Kingman, Arizona
in 1959 when I was on the road.
The best home fries in Boston today
can be had at Sunday brunch at Country Life,
the vegan place near Quincy Market.
(Just know you won't get real eggs
or real coffee with them—
tradeoffs.)

I've fallen for Lyonnaise,
au gratin, DelMonico potatoes,
often delicious once;
baked potatoes, foil-wrapped in restaurants,
sometimes so waxy-succulent
you have to eat the skin as well,
and end up getting foil between your teeth.
But when you go back anticipating,
they never quite live up to recollection.

My wasp brother-in-law argues
that the potato has no taste at all,
it's just a vehicle for butter and salt,
chives and sautéed onions,
cheese and sour cream.
For foil.

But I suspect some temperament
in the potato,
some secret moon under which
it insists that it be picked,
some labor of love, or song,
some sacrifice,
some bloodshed it demands.

IV

I've been a Potato Person all my life.
It started with college loans,
then car loans.
We always had a budget—we'd withdraw
so much a week, and not a penny more—
and we never overdrew.
But neither did we ever go the full
seven days between withdrawals.

And always reason to believe
tomorrow there'll be plenty,
and debts incurred today
will look like    small potatoes.
Meanwhile we're the tuber from which
they draw blood every month.

And at those moments when we see
with absolute crystal clarity
that the system wasn't designed
with us in mind
we hit the road.

Because, hey,
we didn't make the world.

When what we really need
is to raise our voice;
what we really need
is that Good, Sharp Knife.

# I Marched With Martin

My wife and I've had curious experiences before
with synchronicity and dreams,
but this was different,
this raised the hairs on the back of my neck
like a fey cold wind from an unexpected quarter;
this felt of something large and strange at work.

I.

I marched with Martin, but it was late;
not in the sea-change of Selma and Montgomery,
not facing dogs or getting slammed and soaked by hoses—
although I had paid some small dues in Alabama.
Not in the Poor People's March that flooded Washington:
never been poor, just always broke...

No, I didn't seek Martin out,
I waited for him to come to me,
his visit to the relative backwater safety
of Northampton, Massachusetts,
a month or two before Memphis.
We got recruited thinking we
were standing up for civil rights,
then when we got to Northampton
all the signs were about the war,
and we weren't clear yet where we stood on Viet Nam—
but we weren't about to pass up a good march.
"What are you rebelling against?"
"What've you got?"

I suppose that Martin must have spoken,
but all that I remember from that day
is the yahoos in their old sedans
with tailfins, gliding by, yelling
"Nigger-lover," "Draft-dodger,"
thinking somehow to insult us.

I had my own dream that day,
that I would found a flying squad
that would travel the country
protecting non-violent marchers everywhere;
hard young men carrying ax-handles,
commanding from the yahoos some respect.
The ax-handle would be my symbol.

I spoke to a girl about my flying squad,
and she suggested gently that perhaps
I didn't yet quite understand non-violence.
I knew that she was right, knew it the way
that you believe a science teacher who
tells you sound travels better through water;
you believe it even though it doesn't fit
your feel for how things ought to work.

My dream came to nothing, I forgot about it.
But then, we're not much closer to Martin's, either.

II.

In my morning meditation before I wrote this,
that long-forgotten event swam up into consciousness
from the direction of the place where poems hide,
and I promised myself that I would write it,
expecting that it ended with that easy,
cynical line about Martin's dream.

But about the time I pushed myself up
out of my chair and turned on the light,
Carol came out of the bedroom and bleary-eyed began
relating the dream she'd just awakened from,
message from the deep water of her unconscious,
a dream in which I had brought her to a restaurant
that hung out over the ocean on a height,
like a palisade.

Looking down from the restaurant windows,
we could see nothing but white raging surf,
so deeply had tides undermined the sandy cliff.
In her dream, Carol was frightened,
wanted to go somewhere else.
Making matters worse, this restaurant
was full of rednecks, drinking, raising hell,
exuberant in the foreplay of violence,
the combination of man and mood
that always has alarmed her.
Like her father, the prospector.

Waiters were trying to keep the peace,
and as she told this part of her dream
I mused obliquely that the Latin word for waiter
is "minister." (Sometimes the clues to dreams
are things we didn't know we knew.)

In her dream, Carol kept asking herself,
"Why has Jack brought me here?
Why is he making me stay?  And above all—"
and this was the part that chilled me
like a draft from the direction of a wall
that I had always known as windowless—
"above all," she said she thought in her dream,

"why is Jack carrying that ax?"

III.

We tend to remember Martin as civil rights leader,
forgetting that in those last months
he spoke out against the war
before a lot of us were ready to listen.
No matter we resist it,
there is this about the Great Ones,
that they will not be pigeonholed,
they keep moving and growing;

just when we think we understand them
the needful wind shifts
and they're off on a new tack—
and they do not keep still,
and they will not keep still.

One of the Great Ones,
even after he'd been dead a long time,
might still have the power—
especially if he'd been a minister—
the power in a voice that carried
through the deep water of the unconscious,
power to say directly to a heart,

"Today the violence that has to end
          is inside you."

*In Massachusetts there's a controversy raging over
the MCAS tests, a series of standardized tests that
Massachusetts students have to pass before they
can get a high school diploma.*

## THE WHOLE CHALUPA

So I'm on my way to work
jumping around the AM dial, trying to
get last night's Sox score from the coast
and I hear these two guys talking about
the Drop the Chalupa commercial

and I stop and listen because I think
it's one of the funniest commercials I've ever seen
but that's not what these hockeypucks are saying,
no, they're complaining about that commercial
because they don't *get* it....

And even before I can hit the scan button again
Beavis and Buttahan are onto capital punishment
and why am I not surprised that they're
in favor of it? But I am surprised
that they have the *cojones*

to express an opinion on it
right after they've just admitted
*they don't get Drop the Chalupa....*
But isn't this characteristic of us right now?
We live in the Golden Age of the Opinion.

No knowledge, no education, no qualification,
just give us your opinion,
like a judge in a poetry slam....
And even though I like that commercial,
don't get the idea that I'm defending advertising.

The other day I was waiting for the subway
and next to me there's this kid in a GAP sweatshirt
and I said, "How much do you get for that?"
and he said what? and I said "I'm not proud
money's a little tight right now

paying off all those college loans
I wouldn't mind a few extra bucks.
So how much do you charge the GAP
for wearing their advertising like that?"
and he started moving away

from me down the platform, and I yelled,
"I got just one word for you, kid: *MCAS!*"
and he started to run, and all the kids
on the platform started to run away from me
as I stood there shouting "*MCAS! MCAS!*"

Which set me thinking that if I'd stayed with
the Drop the Chalupa guys five more minutes,
they probably would have been ranting and raving
about the schools and the teachers
and *why can't kids pass the MCAS?*

Maybe they can't,
you Twin Peaks of nincompoop,
but I guarantee you
*they get Drop the Chalupa.*
So *why* can't kids pass the MCAS?

Because they don't do any homework.
Why don't they do any homework?
Because they're all out working at Taco Bell.
Why? Because they've become
the hottest market for all the advertisers;

because they have to shell out
48 bucks for a GAP sweatshirt

18.98 for the new Britney Spears CD.
I bought Don't be Cruel for 89 cents.
Hallelujah I Love Her So, Ray Charles,

changed my life, 89 cents. Mack the Knife,
the Louie Armstrong version;
I laid a crumpled dollar down,
they gave me back a penny and a dime,
and they didn't need a calculator to do it.

These kids have buy the whole CD,
and they have to work half a day for that.
Homework pays *nada*,
and they're consumers now.
That's their role in society;

they know it. We just haven't
gotten around to admitting it.
Now you're going to tell me that
they don't have to listen to commercials
and you're right, except for one thing:

advertising works. Every once in awhile
the stakes get high enough to compel us
to acknowledge that it works; we took liquor
commercials off TV, and cigarettes.
We force them to put in disclaimers:

"*Please chugalug responsibly,*" "*may cause
drowsiness, anal leakage, and agonizing death.*"
What we really need is a disclaimer
that says, "I got paid big bucks
to tell you that about Doritos.

If you believe one word I said,
you'd be safer going to
Hannibal Lecter's for an intimate dinner

than you are watching TV because
the advertisers will eat you *alive.*"

Even that might not be enough;
We've made TV the babysitter
for two generations of our kids;
now we find out that was like putting
Dubya in charge of the evidence

in a coke bust. And nobody
understands the power of advertising
better than the politicians,
who gave away the airwaves in the first place.
Now it's poetic justice that

they have to sell their soul
every couple of years
to buy their office back.
Campaign Finance Reform?
Why don't we just say

political ads are free?
Can't we do that?
Don't the airwaves belong to the people?
I'll have to call the Drop the Chalupa guys
and see if they have an opinion about that.

But of course they'll have an opinion about it.
As soon as they *hear* it, they'll have an opinion.
Because you see this bone here?
Note how it goes directly from ear to jaw.
This is the opinion bone.

An idea enters at the ear,
and this bone carries it straight to the mouth,
where it exits matched randomly
with one of three opinions:
it's cool; it sucks; or, for anything

in a gray area, it
         doesn't suck.
The brain never has to be engaged.
In wrong hands, this bone is still
the most dangerous weapon in the world,

the jawbone of an ass.
And the Philistines have turned it against us.
Of course, that's only
         my
                  opinion.

SAVANTS

If you say to them,
"November 6, 1904?"
they will answer, "*Tuesday*,"
and they are always right.

"Calendric savants," they're called,
a subset of idiot savants.
Usually they're retarded,
frequently autistic,
but they have this one curious skill,
infallible.

How would their talent work?
I picture something
whirring in the mind
as in an old movie,
pages of a calendar
flipping to indicate passage of time
but calibrated,
abacus-like, till, "*Saturday*.
Pretty smart, aren't I?"

"You sure are,"
and I can almost believe
that it's just some weird skill,
like Professor Backwards,
except that in 1582
when the calendar went from Julian to Gregorian
ten days in October were skipped
arbitrarily—

and if you ask the savants
for a date in September, 1582,
they *get it right*,
they *adjust* for the missing days.

Explain *that* with your
flipping Franklin Planner.

What do calendric savants answer
when the given date
*is* one of the missing days?
Probably, "*Never.*"

How to explain their talent?
I think some laughing god
encoded a riddle in their DNA
for the rest of us to worry at.
I think the answer to the riddle is,
"*Never.*" We're never going to
figure it all out.

Still and all, calendrics are no more
outlandish than our present crop of
politicians, who know intuitive
and speak upon request
precisely those half-truths
that fifty-one percent
of voters arbitrarily
want to hear.

"Tax cut. Welfare reform.
There is no class war.
*First Tuesday in November.*
Pretty smart, aren't I?"

## SONG OF THE OPEN MIKE

When Seth played his né
in the open mike at the Music City Café
we recalled his telling us
the long, slow process it had been
to win the instrument's consent

to utter any sound at all;
because it seemed at first as though
this would be a throw-back to that
earlier time; he tried and tried to blow,
but no sound came and so

he called for water, sipped
a moment while the audience shifted
and whispered like fallen leaves,
then picked it up again
and strained down into it

looking a little desperate
till finally the long flute sounded
and the audience went silent
from embarrassment to respect
at the long slow notes, like...

whales. Like nothing I had ever heard
except the songs of whales.
And no one knows why whales sing so.
Only that their songs are long and slow
and they never repeat the chorus

exactly the same way twice.
Whales have large brains,
much larger than they would seem to need
for lives that with all due respect
must be described as simple:

swim, swallow plankton, surface every so
often to breathe and blow; once in a great
while, mate. When you feel sand pushing you
up out of the water, *back off.*
Have I left out anything?

It's a principle of evolution that
things unnecessary for survival fall away.
So what's the point of all that brain?
Well, there's another principle that says
when you've got two unanswered questions

try letting one answer the other;
and some scientists have suggested that
perhaps the big brain and the long song
are *connected.* I like that idea.
There are chambers in my brain

that went unopened until poetry.
I can survive from nine to five
without using everything between my ears—
hey, some of my ideas endanger *me.*
A while back my co-workers were going

out to celebrate meeting in October
our target profit for the year and I
wanted to shake them and say, "*Listen,*
this is a celebration of the combination
of how much we do and how little they pay.

"Why don't we work for half as much?
Then we could celebrate in May."
But I back off, till I get here, where
such ideas won't get me fired. If whales
were people they'd be here too, listening

to our long, slow, necessary songs;
being politically correct,
applauding ideas of mutual respect,
like...well, like Save the Whales.
This the song I heard in the open

mike at the Music City Café
when Seth played his né—
Seth, never known to play
*anything* the same way
twice.

## KENMORE SQUARE

I knew a poet who would make
a couple hundred copies of a poem
and stick them in a pouch,
like a mailman
who wrote all the letters himself.

Saturday mornings
he would walk Commonwealth Avenue
from the Public Gardens
all the way to Kenmore Square.
He'd smile at everyone he met,
and offer each a poem.
Most people accepted them.

At Kenmore he would turn
and start back Commonwealth,
conscientious to retrace
the same side of that
gracious boulevard,
and he would reclaim his poems
from the sidewalks and the gutters
where they'd been discarded,
and he would stuff the pieces
back in the pouch.

We watch others go through life
leaving bodies strewn behind
and wonder vaguely
what our own trail looks like.
Bless those brave enough
actually to walk
that backward track.
They walk it for us all.

# SALTPETRE AND ROBERT FROST

At the boys' school I attended
we all believed the legend
of saltpetre in the mashed potatoes.
The salt was said—as when grease fires
flare in kitchens—to deaden the unruly
flames of forbidden sexuality.
But if saltpetre was there truly,
it was notable for ineffectuality.

This was the same school where
they brought in some big names—
Oppenheimer, Robert Frost,
legends in their own lifetime—
to spend a week on campus in
the "Visiting Fireman" program.
They'd sit with us in class
and meet with small groups

of hand-picked students—
myself included—who,
with all roads open, asked
only the most general questions,
the vaguest of directions.
Frost was old, gentle,
white-haired, ever respectful
of us, but had an air as though

always holding back a laugh
at some constant running joke
as if his intercourse with us
was just a playful fragment
of an ongoing dialogue
between two lovers, the way
you'd sit a three-year-old
on your knee and tell her

in her mother's hearing she
would be even more beautiful
than her mother, if only such
perfection were possible, and the words
are heartfelt appreciation,
the hyperbole is slight;
the lovers' joke is in
the indirection.

Some people ask me today,
"Why do you write poetry?"
Sometimes I say to them
that it's my Irish blood;
other times I tell them how I shook
the feathery, parchment hand of
Robert Frost when I was seventeen,
maybe something took.

But if I say that, they ask
why I lost so many years
before I started writing.
Sometimes I answer that I counted cost;
other times I tell the legend
of saltpetre past, highlighting
the fact that it and Frost
kicked in at last

about the same time.

## California Morning

Under a hot white August sky
I was sitting on my new sister-in-law's deck
looking out over a ravine
savoring my first cup of coffee
and three hours time difference
calling what I was doing "meditating"
which meant that nobody would bother me
when a coyote appeared
ambling up a path out of the ravine
in my general direction.

A rabbit popped out of the brush between us
saw the coyote
nothing between them but fast lane
froze into his clump of brown grass imitation.

Coyote stopped too although he gave
no indication he had seen the rabbit.
No it was some rare quality in
the morning air he stayed to savor.

Over the next ten minutes coyote got interested
in creatures and events invisible to me
at every compass point except the rabbit's
took maybe a dozen steps
none of them actually *toward* his
motionless potential breakfast special
yet each oblique step
narrowing the distance between them
by a margin discernible only
to an old geometry teacher

till suddenly
on no trigger I could see
maybe just some natural version
of a three-second violation—

*it ain't that you're too close*
*but it's been too long*
*since you been far enough away—*
breakfast beat a fast break
back into the brush
      and coyote
never a look after him
resumed his stroll
as if knowing all along
it was too much to hope for
but    hey

it's a numbers game
and sometimes
after all the indirection
sometimes
just often enough to keep you coming back
you *do nail something just right.*
I lifted my cup in toast to a *poet.*

## FINTO, FINTARE

*for Steve, who does this, and for Phil*

I woke up 4 AM
from a dream of coining a Latin verb
the way men who have gambled their lives
for a chance to serve God
actually make words up
in the bowels of the Vatican
in order that pronouncements might be made
in a dead language
about occasions of sin
implicit in emerging technologies

"Television" is rendered something like
"*that which is seen over a distance*
*by means of electricity*"
and electricity itself comes out
"*the lightning that runs through wires*
*almost at the same time.*"

In my dream I took the slang word "*fin*"
(for five-dollar bill)
and the Latin verb suffix "-*to*"
which means that what is being done
is being done repeatedly or intensely
and I created "*finto, fintare...*"
which could only mean
"*habitually to pay for things*
*with five-dollar bills.*"

Being awake, I went to the bathroom.
Latin always had a word for that.

Maybe it was a career-guidance dream.

## THE SPACES BETWEEN

*for Helen*

It hurts
      when love dies.
When love is deep
      it hurts deeply
more deeply maybe than you thought
anything would ever hurt
      again.

But with time
the spaces between the moments when it hurts
      get longer
the moments themselves become
      less devastating
till eventually you come to associate them
      with a sad sweetness
that has as much in common with love
      as it does with grief.

I will not say
      *Don't grieve for me—*
do I look like Saint Francis?

But I wish you long
      spaces in between,
and may you carry into them
      all of that sweetness
and only enough sadness to attest

the risk that's being taken
      by everyone who loves *you.*
Every time we love we're saying,
      *Let it ride*
and what's on the table
      is the rent money.

And every time we stride again
out into the crisp desert night
our fists shoved deep into empty pockets
we know ourselves for losers.

But, *Jesus*,
        what brave losers we are.
I wish you this too,
for the spaces in between,
        this bravery.

Jack McCarthy is a Boston-area working guy who's been writing poetry since the mid-60's. He'd been averaging about a poem a year until 1992-93, when two things happened. First, his new wife Carol blackmailed him into attending a workshop with Galway Kinnell; then he brought his daughter Annie, for her birthday, to the open mike at the Cantab Lounge in Central Square, Cambridge, hoping she'd get excited about poetry. Jack was the one who got hooked.

Since then he's brought out a book of poetry (*Grace Notes*), two chapbooks (*Actual Grace Notes* and *Too Old to Make Excuses (But Still Young Enough to Make Love)*), a 60-minute cassette tape (*Poems for Hannah*), and a CD (*Breaking Down Outside a Gas Station*). He was a member of the 1996 Boston National Slam Team, and was an engaging minor character in the feature film "Slamnation," which documented those proceedings, and he was a member of the Worcester team at the 2000 National Poetry Slam, where he finished as the 10th ranked individual. He has won several awards in the Boston-Cambridge area. The Boston Globe says, "In the poetry world, he's a rock star." He lives with his wife Carol in New Hampshire.

Some of the poems in this book first appeared in my previous book and chapbooks: *Grace Notes*, *Actual Grace Notes*, and *Too Old to Make Excuses (but still young enough to make love)*.

And some have been previously published in *Back Bay View*, *The Boston Poet*, *Buffalo Head Society*, *Omnivore*, *Psychopoetica*, *The Underwood Review*, and *Xavier Review*.

"Careful What You Ask For" appears in *Poetry Slam, The Competitive Art of Performance Poetry*, an anthology from Manic D Press edited by Gary Glazner.

"Cartalk: a Love Poem" and "Careful What You Ask For" appear in *The Spoken Word Revolution*, an anthology from Sourcebooks Publishing.